HEART

1. Fold the bill in half. Unfold it.

2. Fold the outside edges to the middle.

3. Mountain fold the bottom corners to the middle of the BACK.

4. Shape the top of the heart by folding away the two corners at the top on the outside. Also fold the two loose corners at the middle to the inside. Turn the bill over.

5. The four outside corners are now folded to the back, but you can hide them as follows. Unfold the four triangles and push them in between the two main layers of paper. Let the paper open slightly when you do this. Turn the bill over again.

6. Push the top edge to the inside and crease. Let the paper open up while you do this.

7. Heart.

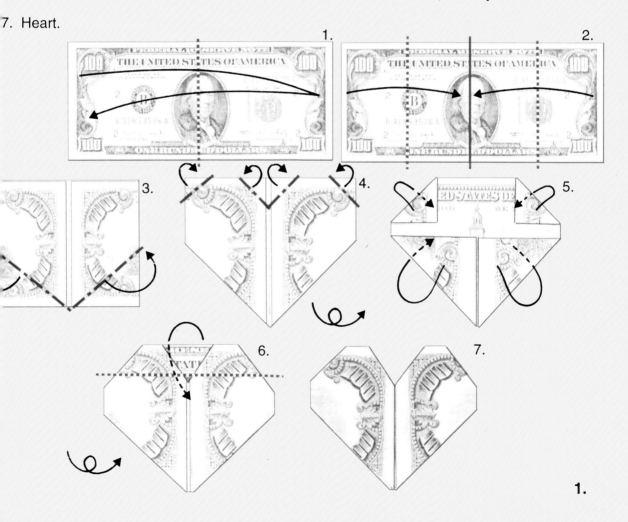

1.

BUTTERFLY

You need:

Two bills
A pipecleaner

Fold one bill as follows:

1. Fold the bill in half lengthwise. Unfold it flat.

2. Fold the long edges to the middle crease. Unfold.

3. Fold the four corners to the middle crease.

4. Fan pleat the bill. Add mountain folds in between the valley folds made in steps 1 and 2. Turn the bill over.

5. Pleated bill.

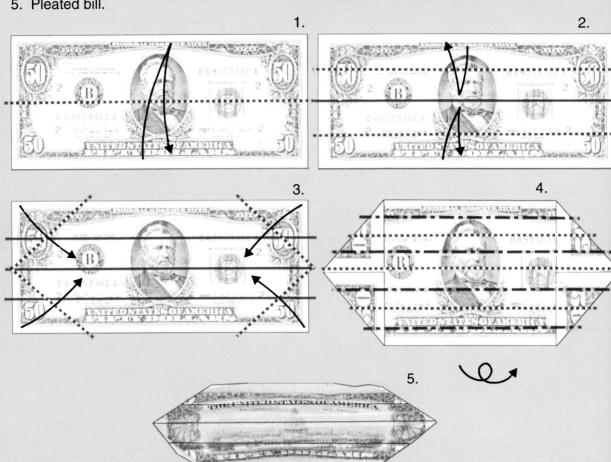

1.

2.

3.

4.

5.

Fold the other bill with this extra step.

6. Before you begin, fold the short edges in about 1/2 inch (1 cm). Then continue with step 1 and all the other steps.

7. Tie the two pleated bills together in the middle with a pipecleaner. Spread the wings. They'll stay in place if you press down to flatten the pleats near the outside.

8. Butterfly.

6.

7.   8.

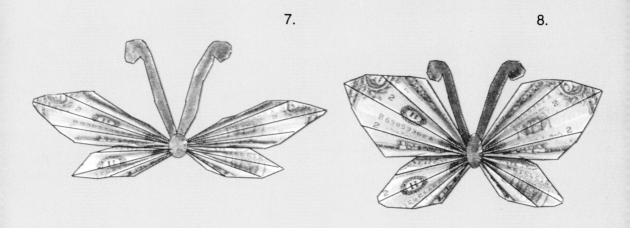

Money Tree

Hang butterflies on a tree made with live branches or wires. Prepare a money tree for a party or shower. Guests can add their own pleated money butterflies as their gifts.

Hair Bow

Create a sensation by putting a money butterfly in your hair!

LUCKY DUCK

1. Fold a bill in half length-wise. Unfold it. Fold two corners to the crease.

2. Fold the slanted edges to the long crease.

3. TURN THE BILL OVER.

4. Fold the two corners to the middle.

5. Fold the bill in half.

6. TURN THE BILL OVER.

In some parts of Asia, a pair of ducks symbolizes a happy marriage because ducks mate for life. That's why ducks are often included in decorations for weddings. Attaching two ducks folded from money bills to a greeting card would be a suitable and unusual gift for a shower, an engagement or a wedding.

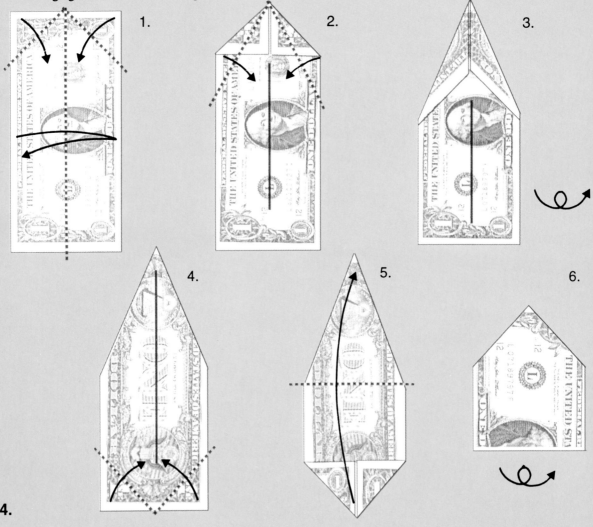

1.

2.

3.

4.

5.

6.

7. Fold the narrow corner to the bottom edge. This will be the duck's head.

8. Mountain fold the bill in half to the BACK.

9. Lift up the back of the head. To make it stay, pinch the front of the body between your thumb and forefinger into sharp creases. See the next graphic.

10. Lift the head away from the neck. Pinch the back of the head sharply.

11. Fold under the tip of the beak to the inside.

12. Lucky Duck.

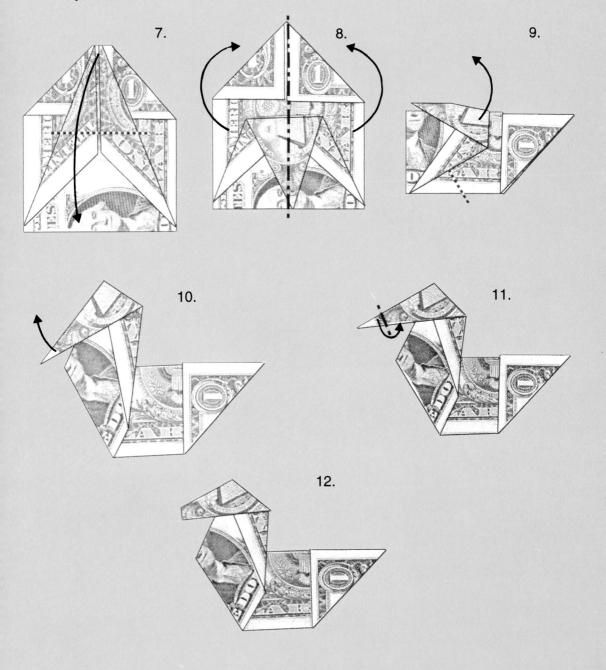

SHIRT

1. Fold up one of the short edges.

2. Fold the bill in half lengthwise. Unfold it.

3. Fold the outside edges to the middle crease.

You may decorate the shirts with ribbon bows, lace, buttons and ties cut from colored gift wrap. Examples are shown in the photo above.

Greeting cards decorated with shirts are welcome on many happy occasions but they are especially appropriate for birthdays, Father's and Mother's Day, new baby arrivals, graduations and retirement parties. Above they have been used on an invitation to a Western Bar-B-Q!

1.

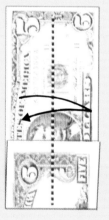

2.

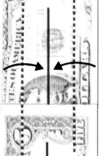

3.

4a. Mountain fold the top of the bill to the BACK.

4b. Flip the two loose corners at the bottom to the outside. Look for the short hidden edge of the bill to begin your creases.

5. Make the collar by folding the outside corners to the middle crease. Leave a gap between the creases for the back of the collar.

6. Slide the bottom edge under the points of the collar and make a sharp crease to keep it in place.

7. Shirt.

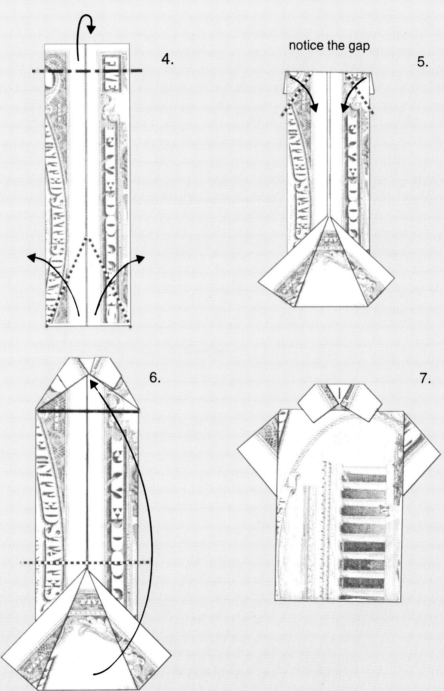

4.

notice the gap

5.

6.

7.

PINE TREE

1. Fold the bill in half lengthwise. Unfold the paper flat.

2. Fold the bill in half by folding the bottom edge to the top edge.

3. Fold the top layer down. See the next graphic for the result.

4. Fold the two corners down.

5. Bring the left bottom corner over. In the process unfold the corner made in step 4 and let it open into a "roof." See the next graphic.

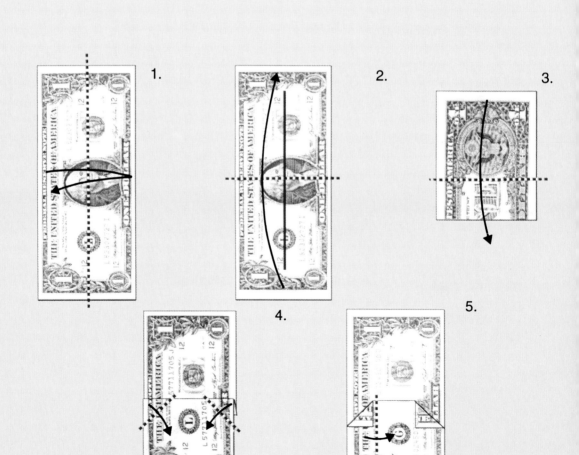

1.

2.

3.

4.

5.

8.

6A. Bring the right bottom corner over to the left in the same way.

6B. Fold the top corners to the middle.

7. Fold the slanted edges to the middle.

8. Back view of the completed Pine Tree. Turn it over to the front.

9. Pine Tree.

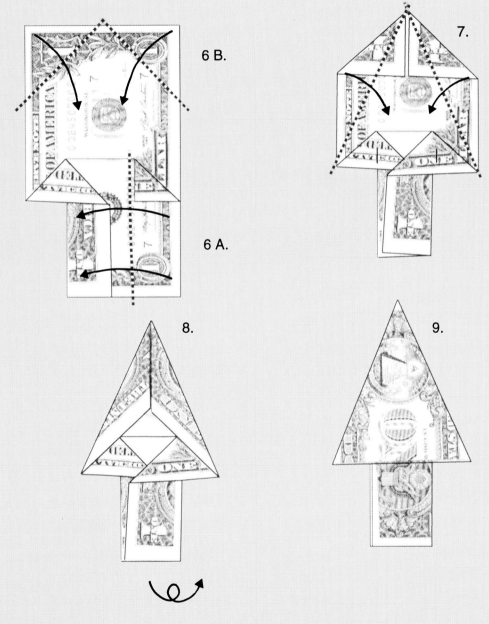

6 B.

6 A.

7.

8.

9.

Use Pine Trees for Christmas decorations and gift tags that are sure to delight.

For table place cards, bend the bottom section of the Pine Tree back and staple it to a piece of cardboard.

FUN RING

It is very important to place the bill exactly as shown in each drawing so that the number appears on the front of the finished ring.

1A. Place the bill with the portrait showing but upside down. Valley fold the long white edges in at the top and bottom.

1B. Fold the bottom edge of the bill to the top edge.

2. Fold the bill in half again but this time from the top to the bottom.

3. Mountain and valley fold exactly in the three places shown.

4. Roll the right side of the strip with the tail over your finger. Then roll the left side on top so that the number shows.

5. Flip the end with the number out of the way to the right.

Anyone who sees you wear the dollar bill ring will be intrigued. The folding sequence is quite complex, but well worth the effort. Once you have practiced a few times, you will be able to do it easily. It will become your own special magic trick. The instructions show how to fold a one dollar bill so that the denomination appears in the middle of the ring. Of course, you may use bills of any denomination.

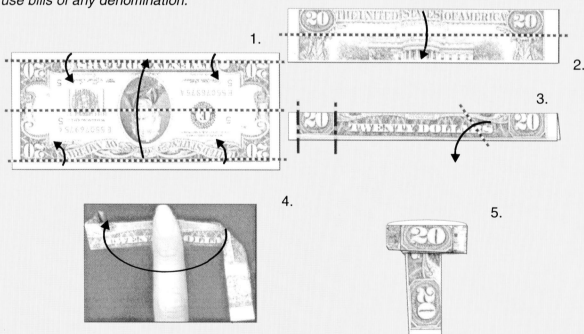

1.

2.

3.

4.

5.

6. Fold the "tail" up.

7. Fold the tail down inside the ring.

8. Fold the short leftover piece of the tail up as tightly as possible.

9. Lock the ring by bringing the number end over and tucking the white edge into the "pocket." You can push it in with the points of a pair of scissors.

10. Dollar Bill Ring.

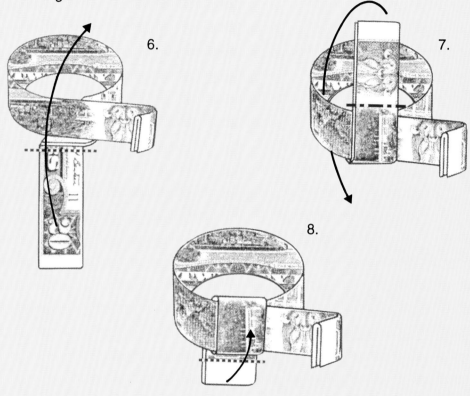

6.

7.

8.

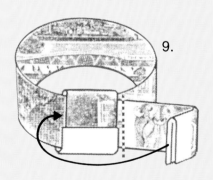

9.

10.

MONEY FOLDING TIPS

Dollar Bills:
Some projects can be enhanced by the design on the bill. For example, the pine tree looks better when the green side is visible. It is vital to follow this procedure with the first step.

Sharp Creases:
Crisp, new bills give the best results. It helps to go over creases with a ruler or popsicle stick.

Temporary Glues:
You can attach folded money bills to cards and wrapped gifts with rubber cement, temporary glue sticks or double-sided sticky tape. Any residue can be rubbed off easily, and the bills can then be unfolded and used.

Gifts:
A greeting card can become a gift when you attach a folded bill to a piece of paper folded in half. It's a welcome way to give presents on birthdays, Christmas, Hanukkah, Kwanzaa, New Year and other occasions.

Money Magic:
Become a magician when you fold money for your friends or relatives. If you want to raise funds for a cause, you can charge a premium for folded money items.